Macrobiotic Desserts

Gourmet sweet foods made without dairy, eggs, sugar, honey, baking powder or soda.

Sandy Shuman

Copyright © 1981 by Sandra Lynn Shuman
All Rights Reserved.
Published by Dictionart, Los Angeles, California
First Printing: January, 1981
Printed in U. S. A.

ISBN: 1-4610-6881-9
ISBN13: 9781461068815

FORWARD

One thing we seem to have a strong attachment to is sweets. And it is understandable when you consider that from the day most American children are born their diet is bombarded with sugar. Along with this sugar most children also get a hefty dose of meat and dairy products.

Why do animal products and sugar go together? Because when we eat animal products, which are a concentrated source of protein, our body craves an excess of carbohydrates for balance. Most Americans satisfy this craving with sugar, white flour products and honey. But eating these foods on a regular basis becomes an addicting cycle of animal products and sweets. It also creates an imbalance in the body which is detrimental to good health. The first step in improving our health is to eat more centering foods such as whole grains and vegetables which are the foundation of the Macrobiotic diet.

I am aware that very few people can change their way of eating in a matter of days, or even weeks. In some cases it is best to take even longer, introducing new foods slowly. Each person will have his or her own transition period. During that period there may be cravings for foods previously eaten. When these cravings are for sweet foods, I offer MACROBIOTIC DESSERTS.

I have also come to realize that many people are not easily satisfied with a simple macrobiotic dessert such as a baked apple, let alone the natural sweetness of brown rice and other whole grains. To these people I offer MACROBIOTIC DESSERTS. And to the people who have been eating macrobiotically for some time, and who on occasion will want to widen their food choices, I offer MACROBIOTIC DESSERTS.

These desserts are good wholesome foods, but as with all desserts they should not necessarily be included as part of the daily diet, though many of us are used to doing so. You might ask, "What's a meal without dessert?". When you eat in a more balanced way, the need for dessert will diminish, and a meal without it can be just as satisfying as one that includes it.

Let moderation and judgment be your guideposts as you journey on the road to good health and prolonged youth.

PREFACE

Macrobiotics is a complicated sounding word that means a very simple thing: living in harmony with the order of the universe. When we are in harmony with this order, we are truly free.

The natural laws of the universe and our response to them effect what happens to us everyday. The understanding and application of these laws can enhance our health and even cure diseases by eliminating their cause. This all begins with understanding the influence of our daily food.

Macrobiotics is a way of eating and thinking that can help us enjoy life with greater vitality and aid us in our continuing development.

The principles of Macrobiotics are thousands of years old. If they were not simple and practical, they would not have endured so many centuries and still be working today.

If you would like to learn more about Macrobiotics, there are many publications available as well as education centers around the world.

The purpose of this book is to present some favorite foods that can be part of a natural transition to a more centered diet, leaving behind such extreme foods as animal products and refined sugar.

ACKNOWLEDGMENTS

I want to thank Roy Steevensz, director of the East West Center for Macrobiotic Studies in Los Angeles, for his inspiring presentation of Macrobiotics, and Marijke Steevensz for her generous teaching and encouragement.

I also want to thank everyone who bought the desserts that I made at the Center, for it was their overwhelming response and enthusiasm that helped me to realize the need for this book.

And a special thank you to Roy Shacter whose love and genius abound throughout this book.

CONTENTS

Forward
Preface
Acknowledgments

Introduction	8
Notes & Hints	9

CAKES
Blueberry Tea Cake	11
Bulghur Cake	11
Creamy Carob Frosting	12
Carob Cake	12
Marbled Brownies	13
Carrot Cake	14
Sweet Cream Sauce	14
Tofu Cheesecake	15
Cookie Pie Crust	15
Corn Cake	16
Tropical Lemon Cake	16
Strawberry Shortcake	17

COOKIES
Chinese Almond Cookies	18
Rugala	19
Buttery Tea Cookies	20
Mondlebroit	21
Tahini Oatmeal Cookies	22
Tamari Roasted Sunflower Seeds	22

MUFFINS & BREAD
4 Grain Miso Muffins	23
Rye Raisin Muffins	24
Pumpkin Bread	24

PIES & PASTRIES
Carob Mousse Pie	25
Oat Nut Crust	25
Chestnut Cream Pie	26
Sour Cream Apple Pie	27

    Light Lemon Pie 27
    Prune Strudel 28
    Spice of Life Tarts 29
    Peach Cobbler 30
    Pecan Pie 31
    Pastry Pie Crust 32
RICE & NOODLE DISHES
    Juicy Apple Rice Squares 33
    Rice Raisin Royale 33
    Walnut Sauce 34
    Traditional Rice Pudding 34
    Fruit Lasagna 35
    Noodle Kugel 36
PUDDINGS, CUSTARDS & OTHER GOOD THINGS
    Vanilla Pudding 37
    Carob Pudding 37
    Toasted Almond Pudding 38
    Caramel Custard 38
    Very Chocolatey Carob Pudding 39
    Carrot Pudding 39
    Zabaglione 40
    Carameled Baked Apples 40
    Carob Fudge 41
AMASAKE
    Amasake Concentrate 42
    Amasake Cupcakes 42
    Maple Tahini Icing 43
    Raspberry Amasake Ice Cream 43
    Amasake Fruit Slush 44
    Amasake Ice Cream Soda 44
    Strawberry Amasake Pudding 45
    Amasake Malt 45
    Carob Amasake Malt 45
    Amasake Café 46
    Hot Amasake 46
    Sweet Brown Rice Milk 47

INTRODUCTION

Macrobiotic desserts are wholesome sweet foods that are made without animal products, refined flour or sugar, chemicals or artificial flavorings. MACROBIOTIC DESSERTS features recipes made with whole grains, the principal food of Man.
It is not necessary to use animal products like eggs, milk, butter or honey, and baking powder, baking soda, refined flour or sugar to achieve sweet and delectable gourmet desserts.
Rather than dairy there is tofu (a soybean product), tahini (sesame seed paste) and whole grain flour! Rather than eggs there is arrowroot and kuzu (starches derived from the roots of these plants) and agar-agar (a sea vegetable). And rather than honey or sugar there are grain sweeteners (rice syrup, barley malt and amasake), pure maple syrup and fruit.
Even though some of these ingredients may be new to you, they are available at health food stores and are easy to use.
I hope you enjoy these sweet foods and that they will help in your transition to a more centered, balanced and healthful diet. I also hope that MACROBIOTIC DESSERTS will inspire you to explore and embrace the macrobiotic way of living and eating, so that one day your main course will be your dessert.

NOTES & HINTS

When I was a little girl one of my favorite stories was THE THREE BEARS. If the three bears were here right now, one of them might say that these desserts are too sweet. One might say that they are not sweet enough. And one might say that they're just right. Whichever "bear" you are, please know that the sweetness of these desserts can be adjusted to suit your taste.

ABBREVIATIONS: c. = cup(s)   w/w = whole wheat
T. = tablespoon(s)
tsp. = teaspoon(s)

BAKING PANS: Place baking pans and cookie sheets that require oiling on top of the stove to warm. A warm pan needs less oil.

BARLEY MALT: Also called Malted Grain Syrup.

KITCHEN EQUIPMENT: I recommend three small investments: a set of 4 measuring cups in increments from 1/4 c. to 1 c. A set of measuring spoons in increments from 1/8 tsp. to 1 T. (When using individual measuring cups and spoons, level off the top with a knife for accurate measurements.) And since all ovens vary, a good oven thermometer is a worthwhile investment for best results.

KUZU: Also KUDZU, is usually in chunky pieces, therefore, it is best to pulverize approximately what you'll need with a small mortar and pestle, or crush with a rolling pin and then measure the exact amount needed. Recipes are based on level teaspoons and tablespoons.

MAPLE SYRUP: Use Pure Grade A Maple Syrup.

OIL: Use unrefined corn, sesame and safflower oils.

CONTINUED ON NEXT PAGE

NOTES & HINTS Continued

ORGANICALLY GROWN: Whenever possible use organically grown fresh and dried fruits, vegetables, grains, nuts and seeds.

RICE SYRUP: Also called Yinnie Syrup and Rice Honey. (If there is a little oil in the measuring cup, the rice syrup and barley malt will come out easily.)

SEA SALT: All salt is not the same. Unrefined sea salt as opposed to refined "table" salt has a much higher nutritional value. And foods seasoned with it have a richer quality to them.

TOFU: Recipes that indicate drained tofu, do not only mean to drain the liquid that the tofu sits in, but to drain the liquid retained in the tofu. To do this, pack the amount of tofu needed into a measuring cup and press out the excess liquid.

UMEBOSHI PASTE: Made from plums which have been pickled in sea salt for up to 2 years.

VANILLA and ALMOND EXTRACTS: They should be Pure Vanilla Extract and Pure Almond Extract without sugar or other additives. Read the label.

The bottom line to these desserts is that the recipes can be followed as written, or serve as a guideline for you to do your own experimenting and make your own discoveries.

CAKES

BLUEBERRY TEA CAKE

1 1/2 c. water
1 1/2 tsp. tahini
1/4 c. corn oil
1/4 c. barley malt
1/4 c. pure maple syrup

2 tsp. pure vanilla
1 tsp. grated lemon rind
3 c. whole wheat pastry flour
1 tsp. sea salt
1 c. blueberries

Preheat the oven to 350°. In a mixing bowl combine the water, tahini, oil, barley malt, maple syrup, vanilla and lemon rind. Stir in the flour and salt and mix well. Add the blueberries and pour into a lightly oiled decorative mold or small cake pan. Bake on the center shelf of the oven for about 55 minutes. Let cake sit in pan for 10 minutes before removing to wire rack or plate to cool further.

BULGHUR CAKE

This unusual cake is made with bulghur (steamed, dried and cracked wheat) which is ground into flour.

2 c. bulghur
1/2 tsp. sea salt
1 1/2 c. water
1/3 c. corn oil

2/3 c. barley malt
1 T. pure maple syrup
1/2 tsp. pure vanilla
    extract

Preheat the oven to 350°. Grind the bulghur into a fine flour. (A blender will do if you do not have a flour mill.) In a large mixing bowl blend the bulghur, sea salt and water. Add the oil, barley malt, maple syrup and vanilla mixing well, working out any lumps in the batter. Pour into an oiled 8 inch round cake pan or a 7 inch soufflé dish and bake for 45 - 50 minutes or until the top is firm and uniformly cracked. Do not overbake. Let cool in baking dish. Remove and frost top and side with Creamy Carob Frosting. (Recipe follows.)

CAKES

CREAMY CAROB FROSTING

1/3 c. roasted carob powder	1 T. w/w pastry flour
1/2 tsp. agar-agar powder	1 c. water
1/4 tsp. sea salt	3 T. pure maple syrup
1/3 c. tahini	1/3 c. barley malt
1/2 tsp. arrowroot	2 tsp. pure vanilla
	1/8 tsp. pure almond extract

In a saucepan combine all the ingredients, except vanilla and almond, and blend well. Bring to a boil, stirring continuously. Reduce heat and gently boil for 5 minutes; stir often. Remove from heat and add the vanilla and almond. When cool, pour into a blender and whip until creamy. Then pour it into a bowl and refrigerate for at least 45 minutes. Spread on cool cake.

CAROB CAKE

2 c. w/w pastry flour	1 1/2 tsp. arrowroot
2/3 c. roasted carob powder	1 c. +2 T. water
2 tsp. sea salt	1/2 c. raisins
1/2 tsp. ground coriander	Creamy Carob Frosting
1/2 c. corn oil	(Recipe above.)
1/2 c. barley malt	35 almonds, thinly
1/3 c. pure maple syrup	sliced and toasted
2 tsp. pure vanilla	

Preheat oven to 350°. In a saucepan combine the raisins and 1 c. of water. Bring to a boil, then set aside to cool. In a large mixing bowl, combine the flour, carob, salt, coriander, oil, barley malt, maple syrup, vanilla and the arrowroot diluted in the remaining 2 T. of water, along with the liquid from the raisins. Mix well. Stir in the raisins and pour into an oiled 8 inch square baking dish or pan. Bake for 1 hour or when center of cake springs back when lightly pressed. Place sliced almonds in oven and toast for about 15 minutes. Remove cake from pan, and cool on wire rack or a plate. When cake is cool, frost top and sides with Creamy Carob Frosting. Press toasted almonds into sides of cake and sprinkle them over the top.

CAKES

MARBLED BROWNIES

1 c. drained tofu	1/2 tsp. sea salt
3/4 c. pure maple syrup	1 1/2 c. water
3 tsp. pure vanilla	1/4 c. tahini
2 tsp. umeboshi paste	1/4 c. barley malt
2 1/4 c. w/w pastry flour	1/4 c. rice syrup
1/3 c. roasted carob powder	1/4 tsp. pure almond extract
	1/2 c. chopped walnuts

Preheat the oven to 350°. Put the tofu, 1/2 c. of the maple syrup, 2 tsp. of the vanilla and the umeboshi paste in a blender, and blend until smooth. Set aside. In a large mixing bowl, combine the flour, carob, salt, water, tahini, barley malt, rice syrup, remaining 1/4 c. maple syrup, remaining 1 tsp. vanilla, and the almond extract. Mix thoroughly. Stir in the walnuts. Set aside 1 cup of this mixture. Oil the bottom and sides of an 8 inch square baking pan. Pour the remaining flour mixture into the pan. Then slowly pour the tofu mixture evenly over the flour mixture, covering it completely. Do not spread it around. Next take the reserved cup of flour mixture and using a tablespoon, drop one tablespoon at a time onto the "tofu" layer in different places. Take a knife and swirl it through to marble. Do not do this too zealously as it will all run together. Bake on the lower shelf for approximately 1 hour or until the center springs back when lightly pressed. Do not overbake. When cool cut into 2 inch squares. Keep refrigerated. Serve at room temperature.

CAKES

CARROT CAKE

2 c. w/w pastry flour
1 c. apple juice
3 T. corn oil
1 c. barley malt
1/2 c. water
2 tsp. pure vanilla
1/2 tsp. sea salt

1/2 tsp. cinnamon
1/4 tsp. nutmeg
1 tsp. fresh lemon juice
1 1/2 c. grated carrots
1/2 c. chopped walnuts
Sweet Cream Sauce (Recipe follows.)

Preheat oven to 350°. In a large mixing bowl combine everything except the carrots, walnuts and Sauce. Mix well. Stir in the carrots and walnuts. Pour batter into a lightly oiled 8 inch square cake pan. Bake approximately 55 minutes. When cool, cut into squares and serve with Sweet Cream Sauce as a topping. Keep refrigerated.

SWEET CREAM SAUCE

3/4 tsp. agar-agar powder
1 1/4 c. + 2 T. water
3/4 c. drained tofu
1 1/4 tsp pure vanilla
3/4 tsp. fresh lemon juice

1/3 c. rice syrup
2 T. + 1 1/2 tsp. pure maple syrup
1/4 tsp. sea salt

Combine agar-agar and 1 1/4 c. of the water in a saucepan; bring to a boil. Reduce flame; simmer 10 minutes. Put tofu in a fine strainer and place in a pot with enough boiling water to cover the tofu. The strainer should rest on the rim of the pot. Turn off heat; let tofu sit for 5 minutes. Remove pot from stove. Take strainer out of the water and with the back of a wooden spoon, press out the water from the tofu. In a blender put tofu, rice syrup, maple syrup, vanilla, salt, lemon juice, agar-agar mixture and remaining 2T. water. Blend until smooth. Chill about 1 hour. (If too thick after chilling, re-blend in blender.) Serve with Carrot Cake and Strawberry Shortcake. Keep refrigerated. Makes 2 c.

CAKES

TOFU CHEESECAKE

1 Cookie Pie Crust
   (Recipe follows.)
1 1/2 c. water
2 tsp. agar-agar powder
2 c. drained tofu
2 T. umeboshi paste

1/4 c. +1 tsp. maple syrup
1/2 c. rice syrup
3 T. barley malt
5 tsp. pure vanilla
2 T. +1 tsp. fresh lemon juice
1/4 tsp. sea salt

Preheat the oven to 350°. Prepare the pie crust. Bake it on the lower shelf for 20 minutes just until the edge is a light golden brown. Remove from oven and let cool 5 minutes. Leave oven on. While the crust is baking, combine the water and agar-agar in a small saucepan. Mix well and bring to a boil. Stir occasionally. Reduce heat and simmer for 5 minutes. In a blender combine the rest of the ingredients, along with the agar-agar mixture and blend until smooth. Be sure to drain tofu well (see Notes & Hints). Pour tofu mixture over the partially baked crust. Return cheesecake to lower shelf and bake it 15-18 more minutes. The top should be a very light golden brown. Do not overbake and allow cracks to form on top of filling. Allow to cool for 1 hour. Then place in the refrigerator 5-6 hours to set, preferably overnight. (The longer it is allowed to set, the better it gets.) Serve at room temperature. Keep refrigerated.

COOKIE PIE CRUST

3/4 c. w/w pastry flour
1 tsp. arrowroot
1/8 tsp. sea salt

3 T. corn oil
2 T. water
1 T. pure maple syrup

Blend all the ingredients in a bowl and press mixture into the bottom only of a 9 inch pie plate. Bake according to recipe directions.

CAKES

CORN CAKE

2 c. corn meal   3/4 tsp. sea salt
2 c. water   1 c. rice syrup

Preheat the oven to 350°. Put the corn meal into an enamel pot and toast it over medium heat for about 5 minutes, stirring constantly. Add the water and cook it for about 10 minutes; stir often. Turn off the flame and stir in the salt and rice syrup mixing well. Oil (preferably with corn oil) a 6 1/2 inch x 6 1/2 inch x 1 1/2 inch baking dish. Pat corn batter into place with moist fingertips. If you do not have a baking dish this size, you can put the cake into a larger dish and with moist fingertips mold it to a shape that will yield a thickness of about 1 1/2 inches. Bake for 20 minutes. Turn off heat, and let cake remain in oven 10 more minutes. Remove and let cool 1 hour before cutting.

TROPICAL LEMON CAKE

1 1/2 c. w/w pastry flour   1 c. rice syrup
1/2 tsp. sea salt   1 T. pure maple syrup
2 T. corn oil   1 tsp. grated lemon rind
1/4 c. tahini   2 tsp. lemon juice
1 c. + 2 T. water
GLAZE:
6 T. rice syrup   2 T. lemon juice

Preheat oven to 350°. In a mixing bowl combine all the ingredients except those for the glaze and mix well. Pour batter into a lightly oiled 8 inch round pan. Bake for 65 minutes or until top is a golden brown. In a small bowl thoroughly blend the ingredients for the glaze and set aside. When the cake is done, let it cool in the pan for 10 minutes. Then transfer to a plate with the crust side up. Immediately, using a spoon, carefully spread about 2 T. of the glaze on top of cake only. The glaze is thin so some of it can be absorbed by the hot cake. (When chilled it will become firm and translucent.) Wait 10 minutes; apply second layer of glaze. Wait 15 minutes and apply final layer. Let cake sit 1 hour. Then refrigerate 1 1/2 hours. Serve at room temperature.

CAKES

STRAWBERRY SHORTCAKE

Its native heritage is American. I read that the New England Indians made an early version of it with wild berries and corn meal. "Genuine" shortcake is a sort of super baking powder biscuit with lots of butter to make it flaky. This recipe is a blending of the two.

          3 cups strawberries   1/2 c. corn meal
          1/4 c. rice syrup   1 1/2 c. w/w pastry flour
          1 1/4 c. water   1/2 tsp. sea salt
          1 T. tahini   Sweet Cream Sauce (Recipe
          4 T. corn oil   is in this section.)

Wash, hull and cut the strawberries in half. Dilute the rice syrup in 1/4 c. of the water and add to the strawberries. Set aside. Combine the remaining 1 cup of water, tahini and oil and chill it in the freezer for 15 minutes. Preheat the oven to 350°. Meanwhile, toast the corn meal in a dry skillet for a few minutes, stirring constantly. Combine the corn meal, flour and salt in a mixing bowl. Remove water mixture from the freezer and mix thoroughly. Slowly blend it into the flour mixture using a fork or wooden spoon. Taking 1/3 cup of the batter/dough at a time, roll it into a ball between your palms. Place it on an unoiled cookie sheet and flatten it to a thickness of 1/2 inch. Bake 20-25 minutes. Tops will not be very brown. (Feel for doneness.) Remove at once to a wire rack or plate to cool. To serve: Place a shortcake in a serving bowl. Top with 1/2 c. of strawberries and some of the juice. Then pour on Sweet Cream Sauce. Serves 6.

COOKIES

CHINESE ALMOND COOKIES

1/2 c. corn oil
3/4 c. barley malt
1/4 c. pure maple syrup
1 1/2 tsp. arrowroot
1/4 c. water

2 1/2 tsp. pure almond extract
3 c. w/w pastry flour
1/4 tsp. sea salt
36 whole almonds

Preheat the oven to 350°. In a large mixing bowl, cream the oil, barley malt and maple syrup by beating them together with a hand beater, wire whisk or wooden spoon. Dissolve arrowroot in the water and beat it into the mixture along with the almond extract. With a wooden spoon stir in the flour and salt. Let it sit 10 minutes. Then shape into 1 1/2 inch balls using 1 level measuring tablespoon of batter. (If batter sticks to your hands, moisten fingertips with a little water before rolling.) Place each ball side by side 2 inches apart on an unoiled cookie sheet. Flatten each ball with your fingertips into a 2 inch round. Press a whole almond gently but firmly in the center of each one. In a small bowl combine the ingredients for the glaze.

GLAZE:
1 tsp. barley malt
1 tsp. corn oil
1 tsp. water

Brush the top of each cookie with a thin film of glaze using your index finger as a brush. Bake the cookies for about 25 minutes or until golden brown. Immediately transfer them to a wire rack or plate to cool. Makes between 32 and 36 cookies.

COOKIES

RUGALA

A Jewish cookie usually made with cream cheese. Here tofu and umeboshi paste are substituted for the cream cheese.

DOUGH:
- 1 c. drained tofu
- 1/2 c. tahini
- 3 T. water
- 1 T. rice syrup
- 1 tsp. umeboshi paste
- 2 c. w/w pastry flour

In a blender put the tofu, tahini, water, rice syrup and umeboshi paste and blend until smooth. Put mixture in a large bowl and using a fork, lightly blend in the flour 1/2 c. at a time. Gather the dough into a ball. Wrap it in wax paper and refrigerate for 30 minutes.

FILLING:
- 2/3 c. raisins
- 2/3 c. water
- 1/4 c. rice syrup
- 1/2 c. walnuts
- 1/4 tsp. cinnamon

While the dough is chilling, put the raisins and water in a small saucepan. Bring to a boil, then simmer 5 minutes. Remove from heat and cool for 5 minutes; drain well and set raisins aside. (Use raisin juice to sweeten another dessert.) Chop the walnuts into small pieces and set aside. Preheat the oven to 350°. Roll out the dough on a wooden board as thin as possible. If dough sticks to rolling pin, sprinkle a little flour over the dough. Using a 9 inch pie plate as a guide, cut out two 9 inch circles of dough. Gather the scrapes into a ball and return to refrigerator. Working with one circle at a time, use a small sharp knife to cut the dough as you would a pie into 16 narrow wedges. Repeat with the other circle. In a small bowl combine the rice syrup and cinnamon and spread the mixture with moist fingertips evenly on each circle of dough. Place several raisins on each wedge, and sprinkle on part of the walnuts. (Remaining ingredients will go over dough still in the refrigerator.)
CONTINUED ON NEXT PAGE

COOKIES

With the aid of a small knife, roll up the triangles. Tuck under the pointed end of each cookie and place them on an unoiled cookie sheet. Repeat same procedure with remaining dough. Bake the cookies for 20-25 minutes or until they are golden brown. Then transfer to a plate to cool. Keep refrigerated. Makes about 4 dozen cookies.

BUTTERY TEA COOKIES

1 1/3 c. w/w pastry flour
2 tsp. arrowroot
1/4 tsp. sea salt
1/3 c. corn oil

1/4 c. water
3 T. pure maple syrup
1/4 tsp. pure vanilla

Preheat the oven to 350°. In a mixing bowl combine all the ingredients; mix well. Take 1 level measuring tablespoon of batter and roll it between your palms into a ball. Place it on an unoiled cookie sheet. With your fingertips flatten it into a 2 1/4 inch round. For a decorative touch score the top of each cookie with the tines of a fork making a plus sign. Bake for about 30 minutes or until the tops are golden brown and the edges a deeper golden brown. With a spatula transfer at once to a wire rack or plate to cool. Makes a baker's dozen.

COOKIES

MONDLEBROIT

In Yiddish mondle is a nut and broit means bread. Traditionally a sweet, nut bread, but more like a crunchy cookie.

1/3 c. raisins	1/3 c. barley malt
1/2 c. water	1/3 c. rice syrup
3 c. w/w pastry flour	1 T. pure vanilla
1 tsp. sea salt	1 1/2 tsp. arrowroot
2/3 c. corn oil	20 pecans chopped
1/3 c. pure maple syrup	

Preheat the oven to 350°. Place the raisins and 1/4 cup of the water in a small saucepan. Bring to a boil and then remove from heat. Let it sit 5 minutes and then drain. (Use raisin juice to sweeten another dessert.) Combine the flour, salt, oil, maple syrup, barley malt, rice syrup, vanilla and the arrowroot dissolved in the remaining 1/4 c. of water in a large mixing bowl. Blend well. Stir in the raisins and pecans. Put the batter in the refrigerator for 10 minutes. Then lightly oil a cookie sheet using your fingertips to spread it. Without washing your hands, take half of the batter and form it into a loaf approximately 9 1/2" long, 3 " wide and 3/4" high. Put it on one side of the sheet allowing room for it to expand. Repeat with remaining batter. Bake in the center of the oven for 55 minutes. Remove from the oven and with a knife carefully make diagonal cuts 1 inch apart and then one cut down the center of each loaf. Return to the oven and bake 5 more minutes or until loaves are a deep golden brown. Then remove and allow to cool on the sheet 5 minutes. With a metal spatula, transfer a few pieces at a time to a plate to cool further. It will take a few hours before the Mondlebroit acquires its crunchy consistency. Makes about 36 pieces.

COOKIES

TAHINI OATMEAL COOKIES

These crunchy and chewy cookies are made without flour.

2 c. rolled oats
1/4 tsp. sea salt
1/4 c. tahini
3/4 c. barley malt
2 tsp. pure maple syrup
1 1/4 tsp. pure vanilla
3 T. water
1/3 c. Tamari Roasted Sunflower Seeds (Recipe follows.)

First make the Tamari Roasted Sunflower Seeds. Set aside. Preheat the oven to 350°. In a large bowl place the rest of the ingredients and blend well. Stir in the sunflower seeds. Let cookie batter sit at least 1/2 hour. Lightly oil (preferably with sesame oil) a cookie sheet. Drop cookies by the spoonful onto the sheet. Shape into a medium thick round about 2 inches wide. Bake for 25-30 minutes, or until the cookies are a light golden brown. Do not overbake. Remove from oven and with a spatula quickly and gently transfer to a wire rack or plate to cool. The centers will be soft, but will become firm when cool. Makes over 1 dozen.

TAMARI ROASTED SUNFLOWER SEEDS

Put desired amount of sunflower seeds in a skillet. Roast them over a medium flame, stirring continuously, until lightly browned. (5-10 minutes depending on amount.) Spray or brush on tamari (authentic soy sauce). They should taste lightly salted. This procedure can also be used to roast pumpkin seeds, almonds and peanuts. (It's worth the investment in an all-purpose spray bottle, not only for tamari roasted seeds and nuts, but to spray tamari on vegetables, etc.)

MUFFINS & BREAD

4 GRAIN MISO MUFFINS

These muffins are so sweet you would think a sweetener was added. Not so. The sweetness comes from the grains, miso and onions. These special muffins can be served with a meal or as a dessert with tea.

1/2 c. millet	2T.+ 1 heaping tsp. Mellow White Miso (Soybean Paste)
3 c. water	1 T. tahini
1/2 c. corn meal	1/4 c. onions, finely chopped
1/4 c. sweet brown rice flour	1/2 c. Spring w/w flour

Put millet in a fine strainer, rinse well under cold water and drain. Put it in a pot with 2 cups of the water, cover and bring to a boil. Reduce heat and simmer until all the water has been absorbed. Preheat the oven to 350°. In another pot combine the corn meal and rice flour and toast it over a medium flame for 3 minutes, stirring constantly to prevent burning. Add the remaining 1 c. of water and cook it for 3-4 minutes until it is very thick and easily pulls away from the side of the pot; stir constantly. When the millet is cooked, remove from heat and let it sit covered for about 5 minutes. Then place it in a large mixing bowl. Add the miso, tahini and onions and mix well. Add the corn meal mixture and whole wheat flour and blend thoroughly. Spoon into a well oiled muffin tin. (Use sesame or safflower oil.) Bake 55-60 minutes or until the tops are golden brown. Let muffins cool in tin for at least 15 minutes. Cut around edge with a sharp knife and remove to wire rack or plate to cool completely. Makes 10 muffins.

MUFFINS & BREAD

RYE RAISIN MUFFINS

3/4 tsp. caraway seeds
1/2 c. raisins
2 c. water
1 c. (Spring) w/w flour
1 c. rye flour

1/2 tsp. sea salt
1 tsp. cinnamon
1/3 c. barley malt
2 T. sesame oil

Preheat the oven to 375°. Combine the seeds, raisins and 1 c. of the water in a saucepan. Bring to a boil; stir occasionally. Reduce heat and simmer for 5 minutes. Set aside to cool. In a bowl combine the flours, cinnamon, salt, remaining cup of water, barley malt and oil. Mix well. Add the raisin mixture and blend well. Fill muffin tin with batter and bake approximately 30 minutes or until done. Tops will be a rich brown. Cool in tin 5 minutes. Then remove to wire rack or plate to cool. Makes 12 muffins.

PUMPKIN BREAD

A very moist dessert bread that lends itself to be sliced and toasted under the broiler or in a skillet. It is made with a Kabocha pumpkin. A Kabocha is green and usually quite sweet. Sometimes it is so sweet, that a slice of it is a dessert all by itself. If you do not use a Kabocha, you will have to add more sweetener.

2 c. Kabocha pumpkin
2/3 c. barley malt
1/2 tsp. allspice
1/4 tsp. ground ginger

1 T. sesame oil
1/2 tsp. sea salt
1 c. (Spring) w/w flour
1/2 c. brown rice flour

In a pot put a washed Kabocha, which has been rubbed with a little oil. Fill pot to a depth of 1/2 inch with water. Cover and cook over a medium flame until soft. When cool, scoop out seeds. Mash pumpkin with skin. In a bowl combine the other ingredients along with 2 c. mashed pumpkin. Put in an oiled loaf pan; bake in a preheated 350° oven for 1 hour. Let it sit for 1 hour before removing from pan. Let it sit several more hours before eating. Keep refrigerated.

PIES & PASTRIES

CAROB MOUSSE PIE

1 tsp. agar-agar powder
1 1/2 tsp. arrowroot
1/8 tsp. sea salt
3 T. tahini
2 T. roasted carob powder
1 c. water

1/2 c. drained tofu
1/3 c. barley malt
1/4 c. pure maple syrup
1 1/2 tsp. pure vanilla
12 pecans
1 9 inch unbaked Oat Nut Crust (Recipe follows.)

Preheat the oven to 350°. Put the agar-agar, arrowroot, salt, tahini and carob in a saucepan. Slowly add the water, stirring until well blended. Bring to a boil and simmer for 15 minutes, stirring occasionally. Remove from heat and cool for 1/2 hour. Meanwhile, prepare Oat Nut Crust and bake on the lower shelf 15-20 minutes until edge begins to turn a medium brown. Remove partly baked crust from the oven and set aside to cool for at least 5 minutes. Leave oven on. In a blender, combine the tofu, barley malt, maple syrup, vanilla, and carob mixture, and blend until smooth. Pour it over the pie crust. Return to oven and continue baking on lower shelf 15 more minutes. Chop pecans, place on upper shelf and roast for about 10 minutes. To decorate: sprinkle lots of pecans around the edge, and a few in the center of the pie while it's hot. When the pie is cool, refrigerate at least 1 1/2-2 hours to set. Serve at room temperature. Keep refrigerated.

OAT NUT CRUST

No flour.

1 c. rolled oats
1/2 c. ground walnuts
1/2 c. ground almonds
1/4 tsp. sea salt

1/4 c. water
1/4 c. barley malt
3 T. corn oil

Mix all the ingredients together in a large mixing bowl. Press mixture into the bottom only of a lightly oiled 9 or 10 inch pie plate. Bake according to recipe directions.

PIES & PASTRIES

CHESTNUT CREAM PIE

FILLING:
- 1 3/4 c. fresh chestnuts
- 2 1/2 c. water
- 1 T. agar-agar flakes
- 1 tsp. arrowroot
- 2 c. drained tofu
- 1/4 c. barley malt
- 1/2 c. +4 1/2 tsp. maple syrup
- 1/4 tsp. sea salt
- 4 tsp. pure vanilla
- 1/2 tsp. fresh lemon juice

Wash the chestnuts. Put them and the water in a saucepan. Bring to a boil. Cover and gently boil for 30 minutes. Drain and set both liquid and chestnuts aside. When the chestnuts are cool enough to handle, peel them, reserving 5 for decoration. When water is cool, put 8 tablespoons of it in the freezer to chill quickly for the pie crust. Preheat the oven to 350°. Put the agar-agar flakes, arrowroot and 2/3 cup of water taken from the remaining chestnut water in a pot. Bring to a boil; simmer for 5 minutes, stirring occasionally. Remove from the heat and set aside. In a blender, combine the chestnuts, tofu, barley malt, maple syrup, salt, vanilla, lemon juice, and agar-agar mixture. Blend until smooth. Set aside.

CRUST:
- 1 1/2 c. w/w pastry flour
- 1/4 tsp. sea salt
- 1/4 c. corn oil
- 7-8 T. cold chestnut water

In a mixing bowl, combine the flour and salt. With a fork, slowly mix oil and then the chilled water into the flour mixture. To roll out dough for 9 inch pie plate, see directions for Pastry Pie Crust; recipe is in this section. Bake pie shell for 20 minutes. Remove from oven and set aside, leaving the oven on. Re-blend the chestnut-tofu mixture and pour it into the partly baked pie shell, and decorate with reserved chestnuts. (Sliced or chopped.) Return pie to oven and bake 15 more minutes. Let it cool for 1 hour. Then put it in the refrigerator for at least 2 hours before eating. Serve at room temperature. Keep refrigerated.

PIES & PASTRIES

SOUR CREAM APPLE PIE

1 1/2 c. drained tofu
2 tsp. umeboshi paste
2 T. fresh lemon juice
1/8 tsp. grated lemon rind
1/4 c. +1T. rice syrup
3 T. pure maple syrup
1/4 c. tahini

1/4 c. arrowroot
1/2 c. water
1 tsp. pure vanilla
3 c. sliced apples
1 10 inch unbaked Oat Nut Crust (Recipe is in this section.)

Preheat the oven to 350°. In a blender put all the ingredients, except apples and crust, and blend until smooth. Set aside. Prepare the Oat Nut Crust and set aside. Wash the apples and cut them into very thin half-moon slices. Layer the apples on top of the crust. Pour tofu mixture over the apples. Place pie on lower shelf and bake for 40 minutes, until top is golden brown. Cool completely before cutting. Keep refrigerated.

LIGHT LEMON PIE

2/3 c. arrowroot
2 tsp. agar-agar powder
1 tsp. sea salt
3 1/2 c. water
2 c. rice syrup
4 tsp. pure maple syrup

1/2 c. fresh lemon juice
1 1/2 tsp. grated lemon rind
1 tsp. pure vanilla
1 10 inch baked Pastry Pie Crust (Recipe is in this section.)

While the pie crust is baking, make the filling. In a medium pot combine the arrowroot, agar-agar and salt. Slowly add the water in order to dissolve the arrowroot and agar-agar completely. Bring to a boil over medium heat, stirring often. Reduce the heat to low and simmer for 10 minutes, and continue stirring often. Add everything else except the vanilla; mix well and simmer a few more minutes. Remove from heat and add vanilla; set aside. Remove pie crust and cool at least 10 minutes. Stir lemon filling and pour it into the baked shell. Let pie cool completely and refrigerate for 4 hours or until set.

PIES & PASTRIES

PRUNE STRUDEL

FILLING:
  2 c. unpitted prunes
  1 3/4 c. cold water
  1/4 c. chopped walnuts

DOUGH:
  1 1/2 c. w/w pastry flour
  1/4 tsp. sea salt
  1/4 c. corn oil
  6 T. ice cold water

Before preparing the filling, put 6 T. of water in the refrigerator to chill for the pie crust. Then wash the prunes. Put the prunes and 1 3/4 c. of the water in a saucepan and boil gently until all the water cooks out, about 50 minutes. Remove from heat. When prunes are cool enough to handle, discard pits and dice into small pieces. Set aside. Preheat the oven to 375°. In a mixing bowl, combine the flour and salt. With a fork, slowly mix in the oil, then ice water. The dough should be somewhat crumbly. Gather the dough into a ball. On a wooden board, roll it out as thin as possible into a rectangle approximately 12 inches x 15 inches. Spread the prunes evenly over the dough. Then sprinkle on the walnuts. Using a metal spatula very carefully run the back side of the spatula around and under the dough. I suggest you practice doing this before you spread on the prunes. Starting from the end closest to you, use your hands to roll up the dough as if you were rolling up a rug, easing the dough off the board with the spatula. If during the rolling process the dough should tear just continue rolling, but if it should tear on the final roll, press the dough together with moist fingertips. Trim off the rough ends with a sharp knife, and with a fork, prick a few holes across the top to let steam escape. Lightly oil the center of a cookie sheet and place the strudel on it. Bake on the center shelf for 40-50 minutes or until the crust is a light golden brown. Cool at least 1 hour. Then using a very sharp knife, cut into 1/2 to 3/4 inch serving pieces. Makes about 12-14 pieces.

PIES & PASTRIES

SPICE OF LIFE TARTS

FILLING:
- 1 1/2 c. dried apples
- 1 c. raisins
- 3 c. water
- 1/2 tsp. cinnamon
- 1/4 tsp. nutmeg
- 1/2 tsp. sea salt
- 1 tsp. lemon juice
- 1 tsp. vanilla

Firmly press apples into a measuring cup to get accurate amount. Then place the apples, raisins and water in a saucepan. Bring to a boil, cover and gently boil for 20 minutes. Drain and set liquid aside. In a blender, combine the apples, raisins, cinnamon, nutmeg, salt, lemon juice, vanilla and 1/3 cup or less of the drained liquid to moisten and blend until smooth. Set aside.

DOUGH:
- 3 c. w/w pastry flour
- 1/2 c. corn oil
- 1/2 tsp. sea salt
- 1/2 c. water (maybe less)

In a mixing bowl, combine the flour and salt. With a fork, slowly mix in the oil, then water. The dough should be somewhat moist. Gather it into a ball. Leave it in the bowl and cover with a damp towel. Refrigerate for 20 minutes. Then divide dough in half. Roll half of it out on a wooden board to a thickness of approximately 1/8 inch or less and a width and length slightly larger that the shallow baking pan or sheet you are using. I use a cookie sheet that is 15"x10"x3/4". To lift dough off the board, carefully run a metal spatula under the dough to loosen it. Place rolling pin at one end of the dough and gently and loosely roll the dough onto the pin, continuing use of spatula as needed. Unroll dough onto an unoiled pan. Trim irregular edges so dough lies flat in the pan. Any gap can be filled with trimmed off excess and patted into place with wet fingertips. Spread the filling evenly over the dough. Roll out remaining half of dough and any scraps, using the same procedure as with the bottom layer. Place it on top of the filling, thus creating a "sandwich". Trim and patch
CONTINUED ON NEXT PAGE

PIES & PASTRIES

as necessary. Using a fork, perforate the top layer in a continuous line across the width of the pan. Make these lines 1 inch apart for the length of the pan. Set aside.

GLAZE:
- 2 tsp. barley malt
- 2 tsp. corn oil
- 2 tsp. water

In a small bowl, blend all the ingredients. Brush the glaze over the top layer of tarts with your fingertips. Bake tarts 20-30 minutes or until golden brown. While still hot, take a sharp knife and lengthwise make one cut down the middle. Then make perpendicular cuts across the width of the pan approximately 2 1/2 inches apart. Makes about 12 large tarts.

PEACH COBBLER

This dessert is best during the height of the peach season.

FILLING:
- 3 c. fresh peaches* (about 8 medium peaches)
- 1 c. water
- 1 T. arrowroot
- 1/2 c. rice syrup
- 2 tsp. pure maple syrup
- 1/2 tsp. grated lemon rind
- 4 tsp. fresh lemon juice
- 2 tsp. corn oil
- 1/2 tsp. sea salt

* If peaches are not organically grown, drop them into a pot of boiling water for 10 minutes. Remove from water and when cool enough to handle use a knife to peel off the skins. Thinly slice the peaches into 1/2 moons and set aside. In a large bowl, combine the water and arrowroot and mix well. Mix in the remaining ingredients. Then add the peaches. When all mixed together, pour the peach mixture into a baking dish; set aside while making the batter.
CONTINUED ON NEXT PAGE

PIES & PASTRIES

BATTER:
- 1 c. w/w pastry flour
- 1/2 c. water
- 1/2 tsp. sea salt
- 1/4 c. corn oil
- 1/2 c. rice syrup
- 1 T. pure maple syrup
- 1/2 tsp. pure vanilla

Combine all of these ingredients in the same bowl you used for the filling and mix well. Slowly pour the batter evenly over the peaches. Try doing this by pouring in straight lines across the dish, then in straight lines down. Bake in a preheated 375° oven for about 35 minutes. Serve warm or at room temperature. Keep refrigerated.

PECAN PIE

- 1 9 inch unbaked Pastry Pie Crust (Recipe follows.)
- 2 c. whole pecans
- 2 T. kuzu (See Notes & Hints)
- 1 tsp. agar-agar powder
- 1/2 tsp. sea salt
- 1 1/4 c. water
- 2 T. corn oil
- 1 c. barley malt
- 1/4 c. pure maple syrup
- 2 tsp. pure vanilla

Preheat the oven to 350°. Prepare the pie crust, but before baking it, layer the pecans on the bottom. Then bake on the lower shelf for about 25 minutes, until the pecans are toasted and crust is a light golden brown, but not done. Remove from oven and set aside; leave oven on. While pie crust is baking, put the kuzu, agar-agar and salt in a saucepan. Add the water slowly in order to completely dissolve the kuzu. Then add the oil, barley malt and maple syrup and blend thoroughly. Bring to a boil, stirring often. Reduce heat and simmer for 5 minutes; stir occasionally. Turn off flame; stir in vanilla. Slowly pour filling into pie shell; adjust the few pecans that have moved so they are evenly distributed. Return pie to lower shelf and bake 15 more minutes, making sure the crust doesn't get overdone. Remove from oven and set aside to cool for 2 hours. Then refrigerate for 2 hours or until filling sets. Serve warm or at room temperature.

PIES & PASTRIES

PASTRY PIE CRUST

1 1/2 c. w/w pastry flour	1/4 c. corn oil
1/4 tsp. sea salt	6-7 T. water

Preheat the oven to 350°. In a mixing bowl, combine the flour and salt. With a fork, slowly mix in the oil, then the water. The dough should be somewhat crumbly. Gather it into a firm ball. Leave it in the bowl and cover it with a damp towel. Refrigerate for 20 minutes. Roll out dough to a 10 (or 11) inch round on a wooden board. (If dough should stick to the rolling pin, simply sprinkle a little flour over the dough.) To lift it off the board, carefully run a metal spatula under the dough to loosen it. Place your rolling pin at one end and gently and loosely roll the dough onto it, continuing use of the spatula as needed. Unroll the dough onto an unoiled 9 (or 10) inch pie plate and fit it into place. Prick bottom and sides of the shell with a fork. Bake on lower shelf for about 30 minutes, or until it is golden brown.

IDEA: Roll out any leftover dough and fill with cooked vegetables, grains or beans. Create your own shapes. Bake until crisp and light golden brown. Also, whenever there is a little dough left over, you can put it in a miniature pie tin and reserve a little filling to put in it. This way you can see how it comes out before you serve it. Or if it is not to be eaten soon, you don't have to wait to taste it. There are many benefits to this procedure.

RICE & NOODLE DISHES

JUICY APPLE RICE SQUARES

1 c. short grain brown rice	3 1/3 c. apple juice
4 c. water	1/2 tsp. arrowroot
1/2 tsp. sea salt	1/4 tsp. cinnamon
2 c. firmly packed dried apples	1/8 tsp. nutmeg
	1/4 c. almonds

Wash rice. Combine rice in a pot with water and salt. Cover and start cooking on a low flame gradually increasing heat from low to high. When water starts to boil, reduce heat to a medium low flame and cook until the water has been absorbed and the rice is creamy. Place apples and 3 cups of the apple juice in a medium saucepan. Bring to a boil and simmer until the apples are very soft, about 1 hour 15 minutes. Then dilute arrowroot in remaining 1/3 c. of apple juice along with the cinnamon and nutmeg; add to the apples. Cook 5 minutes more, stirring often. Add apple mixture to cooked rice and mix well. Place in an oiled baking dish approximately 10 1/4"x 6 1/4"x 2". With a very sharp knife thinly slice the almonds and sprinkle them on top of the rice. In a preheated 350° oven, bake it on the lower shelf for 30 minutes. Let it sit at room temperature for at least 2 1/2 hours before serving.

RICE RAISIN ROYALE

1 c. short grain brown rice	1 tsp. sea salt
1 c. sweet brown rice	1 c. raisins
5 c. water	Walnut Sauce (Recipe follows.)

Wash rice. Place in a pot with water, salt and the raisins on top. Cook as directed in Juicy Apple Rice Squares. When cooked, stir gently and place in an unoiled casserole dish. Allow to cool and set. Serve with Walnut Sauce as a topping.

RICE & NOODLE DISHES

WALNUT SAUCE

1/2 c. walnuts, chopped
3/4 c. drained tofu
2 T. tahini
1/2 c. water
2 tsp. pure maple syrup

1/2 c. + 1 tsp. rice syrup
2 tsp. pure vanilla
1 tsp. umeboshi paste
1/4 tsp. sea salt

Place chopped walnuts under the broiler to toast for about 5 minutes. Watch the time. Set aside. Put tofu in a fine strainer and place in a pot with enough boiling water to cover the tofu. Strainer should rest on rim of pot. Turn off flame; let tofu sit for 3 minutes. Remove from stove. Take strainer out of the water and with a wooden spoon, press out the water from the tofu. Set aside. In a saucepan bring the tahini and the 1/2 c. of water to a boil; boil 2 minutes. Stir often. In a blender combine all the ingredients except the walnuts. Blend until smooth. Stir in the toasted walnuts. Pour over individual servings of Rice Raisin Royale. Makes a little over 1 cup.

TRADITIONAL RICE PUDDING

1 c. short grain brown rice
6 c. water
1/2 tsp. sea salt
1/3 c. raisins
1/4 c. whole oat flour
2 T. brown rice flour

1 tsp. agar-agar powder
5 T. pure maple syrup
1 T. rice syrup
1 3/4 tsp. pure vanilla
1/4 tsp. + pinch cinnamon

Wash rice. Place it in a pot with 4 cups of the water and 1/4 tsp. of the salt. Cover and cook as directed in Juicy Apple Rice Squares. Then put raisins in a small saucepan with just enough water to cover; boil 3 minutes. Drain and set aside. In a saucepan combine the flours, agar-agar and 2 c. of the remaining water. Bring to a gentle boil; cook 10 minutes, stirring often. Remove from heat and add the syrups, vanilla, cinnamon and remaining 1/4 tsp. salt. Blend in a blender until smooth. Add this mixture to the cooked rice along with the raisins. Pour into an unoiled baking dish. (Fits nicely into a 1 1/2 qt. loaf dish.) Bake in a preheated 350° oven for 30 minutes or until top is a golden brown. Cool before eating.

RICE & NOODLE DISHES

FRUIT LASAGNA

PART I:
- 1 c. dried peaches diced
- 1 c. dried nectarines diced
- 2 c. dried apricots
- 1/2 c. raisins
- 8 c. water

To get accurate measurement of dried fruit, pack firmly in measuring cup. Put all the ingredients in a large pot and bring to a rapid boil. Reduce heat and boil gently until all the water has cooked out (approximately 1 hour). Set aside and cool.

PART II:
- 8 oz. whole wheat lasagna noodles

Put noodles in a large pot filled with boiling water. Drop noodles in slowly so water continues boiling. Stir briefly with a wooden spoon. Cook for 30 minutes. Do not rinse, just drain the noodles thoroughly in a colander. Set aside. When cool enough to handle arrange noodles on a large plate to keep them flat.

PART III: (Custard)
- 1/2 c. brown rice flour
- 1 c. whole oat flour
- 1 tsp. agar-agar powder
- 5 c. water
- 1/2 tsp. sea salt
- 1/4 c. rice syrup
- 2 T. pure maple syrup
- 1 T. pure vanilla

Put the first four ingredients in a medium large saucepan. Bring to a full boil, stirring constantly. Reduce heat and add the salt and gently boil for 5 minutes, stirring often. Remove from heat and add the rice syrup, maple syrup and vanilla. Cool 5 minutes; pour into a blender and blend until smooth. In a very lightly oiled casserole dish, put alternate layers of noodles, fruit and custard ending with a top layer of noodles. Cover the casserole with foil and Bake in a preheated 350° oven on the lower shelf 25 minutes. Serve at room temperature. Keep refrigerated.

RICE & NOODLE DISHES

NOODLE KUGEL

8 oz. thin w/w noodles
1/2 c. raisins
1/2 c. tofu
3/4 c. barley malt

2 T. tahini
3/4 tsp. sea salt
1 T. pure vanilla
1 1/2 tsp. fresh lemon juice

Preheat the oven to 350°. Cook the noodles in a pot of boiling water until they are soft. Drain the noodles thoroughly in a colander for a few minutes. Do not rinse, and place in a large bowl. Put the raisins in a small saucepan with just enough water to cover. Boil for 1-2 minutes. Pour off liquid and set raisins aside. In a blender combine the remaining ingredients and blend until smooth. Stir the tofu mixture and raisins into the noodles. Pour into an unoiled 1 1/2 quart baking dish and bake on the lower shelf for 20 minutes or just until the top turns a rich light brown. Serve warm or at room temperature. Keep refrigerated.

PUDDINGS, CUSTARDS & OTHER GOOD THINGS

VANILLA PUDDING

1/4 c. whole oat flour
2 T. short grain brown
   rice flour
1 tsp. agar-agar powder
1/4 tsp. sea salt

2 1/4 c. water
2 T. rice syrup
3 T. pure maple syrup
2 1/2 tsp. pure vanilla

In a medium saucepan combine the flours, agar-agar and salt. Add the water and blend well. Bring to a boil; stir often. Reduce flame and simmer for 10 minutes, stirring often. Remove from heat; add remaining ingredients. Put in a blender and blend until smooth. Pour into serving dishes or 1 large bowl. When cool, place in refrigerator for at least 45 minutes before eating. Serve at room temperature. Keep refrigerated. Makes about 2 1/4 cups.

CAROB PUDDING

1/4 c. whole oat flour
2 T. short grain brown
   rice flour
1/2 tsp. agar-agar powder
1/2 tsp. sea salt

2 tsp. roasted carob
   powder
2 c. water
1 T. pure vanilla
3 T. pure maple syrup
2 T. barley malt

In a medium saucepan combine everything except the vanilla, maple syrup and barley malt. Bring to a boil; stir often. Reduce flame and simmer for 10 minutes, stirring often. Remove from heat and add the remaining ingredients. Pour into a blender and blend until smooth. Pour into serving dishes or 1 large bowl. When cool, refrigerate for at least 45 minutes before eating. Serve at room temperature. Keep refrigerated. Makes 2 cups.

PUDDINGS, CUSTARDS & OTHER GOOD THINGS

TOASTED ALMOND PUDDING

Vanilla Pudding (Recipe is in this section.)
1/4 tsp. pure almond
20 almonds, chopped

Make Vanilla Pudding according to recipe directions. After pudding is puréed in a blender allow pudding to cool. Meanwhile, toast the chopped almonds either under the broiler for 5 minutes or in a preheated 350° oven for 12-15 minutes. When pudding is cool, **add** the almond extract and blend again in blender. Turn off blender; stir in toasted almonds. Reserve a few almonds for garnish. Pour into serving dishes and place in refrigerator to set for at least 45 minutes. Before serving sprinkle the reserved toasted almonds over pudding. Serves 3-4.

CARAMEL CUSTARD

1/4 c. whole oat flour
2 T. brown rice flour
2 tsp. agar-agar powder
1/2 tsp. sea salt
2 1/4 c. water
1 T. barley malt
3 T. pure maple syrup
1 T. pure vanilla
CARAMEL:
2 T. barley malt
1 T. pure maple syrup
1 tsp. pure vanilla
1 tsp. water
1/8 tsp. sea salt

In a saucepan combine the flours, agar-agar, salt and water. Blend well. Bring to a boil; stir often. Reduce heat and gently boil for 15 minutes; stir occasionally. Remove from heat. Add remaining ingredients for custard; pour into blender. Blend on high speed for at least 1 minute. Cool 10 minutes. Meanwhile, combine ingredients for Caramel in a small bowl; blend well. Pour 1/2 c. +1T. custard into 4 small bowls. Refrigerate at least 1 hour. Before serving drizzle 1T. caramel over custard. Or if you have four 6 oz. custard cups spoon 1T. caramel into bottom of each cup. Pour 1/2 c. +1T. custard over caramel. Refrigerate to set. To serve run a small knife around edge; turn over into serving dish. Let it sit a minute. Shake cup and remove. Serve at room temperature.

PUDDINGS, CUSTARDS & OTHER GOOD THINGS

VERY CHOCOLATEY CAROB PUDDING

2 T. agar-agar flakes
2 T. arrowroot
1/2 tsp. sea salt
1 1/2 c. water
3 T. +2 tsp. tahini

5 T. roasted carob powder
4 T. +2 tsp. maple syrup
4 T. barley malt
2 tsp. pure vanilla
1/4 c. chopped walnuts

In a saucepan, combine the agar-agar flakes, arrowroot, salt, water and tahini. Bring to a rapid boil, stirring occasionally. Reduce heat and simmer for 5 minutes. Mix in the carob, maple syrup and barley malt and continue simmering for 15 minutes. Stir often. Turn off flame and stir in the vanilla and walnuts. Pour pudding into serving dishes or a bowl. When cool, about 30 minutes, place in the refrigerator for several hours to set. Serves 3-4.

CARROT PUDDING

1 1/4 c.(Spring) w/w flour
1/2 tsp. sea salt
3/4 c. water
2 T. corn oil
1/2 c. barley malt

3 T. pure maple syrup
1 1/4 tsp. grated lemon rind
1 tsp. lemon juice
1 1/4 c. grated carrots

In a mixing bowl combine all of the ingredients and mix well. Pour into an oiled 1 quart ring mold or baking dish. Bake in a preheated 350° oven for 55 minutes. Let it cool in mold for at least 15 minutes before removing to a wire rack or plate to cool. Cool an additional 1/2 hour before cutting. Serve warm or at room temperature. Keep refrigerated.

PUDDINGS, CUSTARDS & OTHER GOOD THINGS

ZABAGLIONE

An Italian wine custard but without egg yolks and white sugar.

    1 c. drained tofu   1 T. barley malt
    6 T. Mirin (sweet cook-   1 T. pure maple syrup
       ing sake/rice wine)   1/4 tsp. sea salt
    2 T. water   2 tsp. pure vanilla

Purée all ingredients, except the vanilla, in a blender. Put the mixture in a saucepan over a medium flame and bring to a boil, stirring continuously. Boil gently 1-2 minutes, until the mixture begins to curdle. Remove from heat and add the vanilla. Set aside to cool for 10 minutes. Return to blender and blend again until smooth. Serve in stemmed glasses or as a sauce over a variety of desserts. Serve warm or cold. (To serve as a sauce, you may have to re-blend it after chilling in order to pour it easily.)

CARAMELED BAKED APPLES

    Apples (use as many as   1 tsp. arrowroot
       you want to serve)   1/2 tsp. sea salt
    water   1 1/4 c. + 1 T. water
          1 T. corn oil
          1 c. barley malt
CARAMEL SAUCE: 3 T. pure maple syrup
    2 T. kuzu   1 tsp. pure vanilla
    1 tsp. agar-agar powder   toasted chopped almonds

Preheat the oven to 350°. Wash and core apples. Place them in a shallow baking dish and fill the dish with water to a depth of 1/4 inch. Bake for 20-25 minutes or until the apples are soft. Meanwhile prepare the Caramel Sauce. In a saucepan, combine the kuzu, agar-agar, arrowroot and salt. Add the water slowly in order to completely dissolve the kuzu. CONTINUED ON NEXT PAGE

PUDDINGS, CUSTARDS & OTHER GOOD THINGS

Then add oil, barley malt and maple syrup. Bring to a boil, stirring often. Reduce heat and simmer for 10 minutes. Stir often. Turn off flame and stir in the vanilla. Makes 1 1/2 c. (Chop and toast the almonds while the apples are baking.) To serve: Place each apple in a bowl and spoon warm Caramel Sauce over it. (If Caramel Sauce sets before you're ready to serve it, simply reheat it.) Top with toasted chopped almonds.

CAROB FUDGE

1/2 c. roasted carob powder
2 T. agar-agar powder
1 tsp. sea salt
1/2 c. tahini

1 c. pure maple syrup
1 T. +1/2 tsp. arrowroot
1/2 c. +1T. water
2 T. pure vanilla
1/2 c. chopped walnuts

Combine all the ingredients, except the vanilla and walnuts, in a saucepan and bring to a boil. Stir constantly. Simmer for 3 minutes; continue stirring. Remove from heat. Stir in the vanilla and walnuts. Pour fudge mixture into a pan approximately 8 1/2" x 5 " x 1". (I found a foil pan (package of 3) at the supermarket that is ideal.) Spread fudge into place with a spatula. Let it sit 20 minutes or until bottom of pan feels cool. Place in refrigerator on bottom shelf for at least 2 hours to set. Cut into squares or cut it as you eat it. Keep refrigerated.

AMASAKE

AMASAKE CONCENTRATE

Pronounced ah-mah-ZAH-kay. This is a lovely sweetener. It is as versatile as it is nutritious. It can be used instead of sugar and honey. And because it is rich in enzymes, it assists the leavening process and adds a nice moistness to breads, rolls, muffins, pancakes and cakes.

    1 c. short grain brown rice,   2 3/4 c. water
        washed and drained   1 c. rice koji

Combine rice and water in a pot, cover and cook over a medium flame for about 1 hour, or until all the water has been absorbed. Allow to cool until slightly warm to the touch. Mix in koji and pack mixture into a glass or porcelain bowl. Cover with a towel and place in an oven with just the pilot light on and incubate for 12 hours. (If you do not have a gas oven, place mixture in a wide mouth jar and cover tightly. Float it in a large covered pot or tub partially filled with warm water, or wrap in towels and place over a hot water heater.) After 12 hours remove rice from oven, place in a pot and bring to a boil, stirring often. Boil gently for 2-3 minutes. Purée in a blender. Put in a glass jar and keep refrigerated. It will keep several weeks.   Makes 2 1/2 cups.

AMASAKE CUPCAKES

    2 c. w/w pastry flour   1/2 tsp. pure vanilla
    1 1/2 c. amasake concentrate   1/8 tsp. pure almond
    1/2 c. water   extract
    2 T. corn oil   1/4 c. sunflower seeds
    1/2 tsp. salt   Maple Tahini Icing
                                         optional (Recipe follows.)

Combine all ingredients except icing in a mixing bowl. Mix well and pour into an oiled muffin tin. Bake 45-60 minutes or until tops are a deep golden brown. Makes 9.

AMASAKE

MAPLE TAHINI ICING

3 T. pure maple syrup
4 1/2 tsp. tahini

2 pinches sea salt

Combine all ingredients in a small saucepan and bring to a boil, stirring continuously. Reduce heat and simmer 3-4 minutes. Remove from heat, cool and spread over the tops of cool cupcakes. (If you want to use this to ice other cakes, the ratio of maple syrup to tahini is 2 to 1.)

RASPBERRY AMASAKE ICE CREAM

1 1/2 c. amasake concentrate
1 T. kuzu (See Notes & Hints)
1 T. tahini
3/4 c. water

1/4 tsp. sea salt
3/4 tsp. pure vanilla
1 c. fresh raspberries or strawberries

Combine the amasake, kuzu, tahini, water and salt in a saucepan. Mix thoroughly, making sure that kuzu is dissolved. Bring to a rapid boil. Reduce heat and gently boil for 5 minutes. Remove from heat and add vanilla extract. When cool, pour into a blender, add washed raspberries and blend until smooth. Pour into a plastic container and freeze. Before eating let it thaw at room temperature for at least 1-1 1/2 hrs. Makes about 2 cups.

AMASAKE

AMASAKE FRUIT SLUSH

Tastes like a creamy sherbet. A great summertime cooler and dessert.

PART I:
 1 c. amasake concentrate* 3/4 c. berries, peaches
 2/3 c. water   OR melon **
 1/4 tsp. sea salt

* Follow same recipe for Amasake Concentrate, but use 1/2 part koji to 1 part rice. ** Try 1/2 c. raspberries and 5 strawberries. Put all the ingredients in a blender and blend until smooth. Pour into an ice cube tray and freeze. When frozen, remove from freezer and let it thaw at room temperature until it's soft enough to be puréed in a blender (about 25 minutes), but still fairly hard.

PART II:
 Put partially thawed fruit mixture in a blender and add:
 1/2 c. amasake concentrate
 1/4 c. water.
Then blend until smooth. About 4 servings.

NOTE: The more amasake concentrate and water you add (2 to 1 as above), the more it will become a fruit milkshake.

AMASAKE ICE CREAM SODA

 Raspberry or Strawberry   Sparkling spring or
   Amasake Ice Cream   mineral water

In a glass, dilute a little ice cream in a little water. Then add desired amount of ice cream and water.

AMASAKE

STRAWBERRY AMASAKE PUDDING

Its color is as delicious as its taste.

>1 box strawberries
>2 c. amasake concentrate
>1 1/4 c. water
>4 tsp. kuzu (See Notes & Hints)
>1 tsp. sea salt
>1/2 tsp. agar-agar powder
>1/2 tsp. pure vanilla

Wash and hull the strawberries. Cut them into quarters, or if large cut them into eighths. Set them aside. In a medium pot, combine the remaining ingredients except the vanilla. Bring to a boil, stirring often. Reduce heat and simmer for 10 minutes, stirring occasionally. Add the strawberries and vanilla. Stir for a few more minutes as the color becomes a rich pink. Remove from heat and allow to cool. Then chill in the refrigerator for at least 2 hours. Serves 4.

AMASAKE MALT

>1/2 c. amasake concentrate
>1/8 tsp. sea salt
>1 c. water (Add more water for less sweetness)

Mix the ingredients in a blender. Pour into a glass jar and keep refrigerated. Shake well before drinking. Makes 1/2 pint.

CAROB AMASAKE MALT

>1 c. amasake concentrate
>1 c. water
>2 tsp. roasted carob powder
>1/2 tsp. pure vanilla
>1/4 tsp. sea salt

Mix the ingredients in a blender. Pour into a glass jar and keep refrigerated. Shake well before drinking. Makes well over 1/2 pint.

AMASAKE

AMASAKE CAFÉ

Remarkably similar to the taste of coffee with cream and sugar. Serve in espresso cups or small glasses. Serves 2.

1/2 c. amasake concentrate
1/2 c. water
1/8 tsp. sea salt
1 tsp. Cafix (brand name of a grain coffee)

Mix all the ingredients in a blender. Pour into a small saucepan and bring to a boil. Stir often. Serve hot. (Served cold it is a delicious coffee malt.)

HOT AMASAKE

A delicious and soothing drink as well as a sweet and simple dessert. Serves 2.

1/2 c. amasake concentrate
1 c. water
pinch of salt
dab of grated ginger

Mix the concentrate and water in a blender. Pour into a saucepan and add the salt. Bring to a boil. Turn off flame and stir in the peeled and grated ginger. Serve in small cups.

AMASAKE

SWEET BROWN RICE MILK

It tastes like milk and can be used as milk.

    1/2 c. amasake concentrate*   1/2 tsp. sea salt
    2 c. water

* Make amasake concentrate according to recipe directions, except use sweet brown rice instead of short grain brown rice. Mix the amasake, water and salt in a blender. Pour into a glass jar or bottle and refrigerate. (Will keep 5-7 days.) Shake well before drinking. Makes 1 pint.

mac·ro·bi·ot·ics the art/ philosophy/science of healing, health and happiness by living in harmony with the order of the universe, and applying the laws of nature especially in the preparation and consumption of our daily food.

CPSIA information can be obtained at www.ICGtesting.com
Printed in the USA
BVOW05s2121120913

331017BV00009BA/361/P